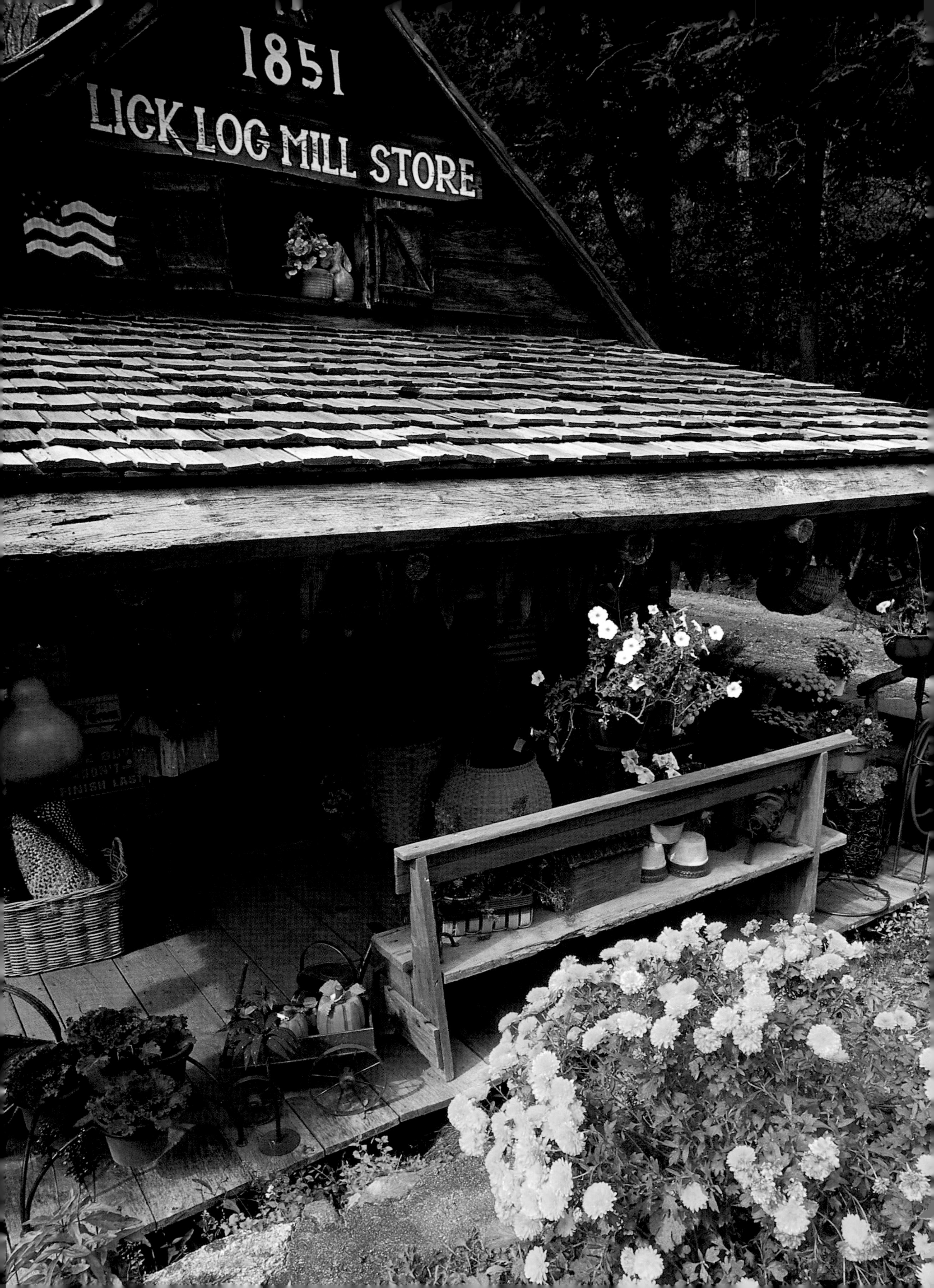
1851
LICK LOG MILL STORE

Our
North Carolina

Voyageur Press

Library of Congress Cataloging-in-Publication Data
Adams, Kevin, 1961-
  Our North Carolina / Kevin Adams.
    p. cm.
  ISBN 0-89658-661-8 (hardback)
  1. Natural history--North Carolina--Pictorial works. I. Title.
QH105.N8A34 2005
975.6'044--dc22

                              2004023375

Published by Voyageur Press, Inc.
123 North Second Street, P.O. Box 338,
Stillwater, MN 55082 U.S.A.
651-430-2210, fax 651-430-2211
books@voyageurpress.com
www.voyageurpress.com

Page 1: *A perfect way to start the day after camping on Mount Sterling's summit in Great Smoky Mountains National Park is to climb the historic fire tower and watch the sunrise over an often fog-filled valley.*

Page 2: *Morning twilight at Cape Hatteras National Seashore has the sky awash in purple, red, and orange light. Despite this "sailor's warning" sky, a red horizon on the Outer Banks is usually a sign of clear weather.*

Page 3: *Accessible only by boat, Ocracoke Island is a favorite destination for those seeking an uncrowded and less touristed beach. Except for the gulls and perhaps an angler or two, you can often have the sunrises to yourself.*

Page 4: *At 411 feet, Whitewater Falls in Nantahala National Forest is often cited as the highest waterfall in the East. This view shows only the smaller upper section of the waterfall.*

Page 5: *The "missing link" of the Blue Ridge Parkway, the Linn Cove Viaduct at Grandfather Mountain was completed in 1987, fifty-two years after construction of the roadway began. Today, the engineering landmark is among the most popular attractions along the entire 469-mile length of the parkway.*

Page 6: *At the Lick Log Mill Store on the outskirts of Highlands, shoppers can browse a variety of goods and explore an old water mill, still standing on the grounds.*

Page 7: *Orton Plantation overlooks the Cape Fear River just south of Wilmington. Originally a rice plantation in the early nineteenth century, the grounds today feature twenty acres of formal gardens. While there is always something in bloom, most people come in April to see the profusion of azaleas.*

Page 8, top left: *Low tide on the sand flats of Cape Lookout National Seashore reveals countless treasures for beachcombers, such as this keyhole urchin, Mellita quinquiesperforata, known to most people as a "sand dollar."*

Top right: *The species name of the coquina clam, Donax variabillis, reflects the shell's seemingly unlimited variety of colors and patterns. Known to many people as the "butterfly shell," the mollusk is a favorite summer snack for shorebirds and the makings for a popular chowder for humans.*

Bottom left: *With the decline of the shrimp and oyster industry, blue crabs, Callinectes sapidus, have become one of North Carolina's most important fisheries. The crustaceans pictured here have just been caught and are awaiting shipment to a processing facility.*

Bottom right: *Hernando De Soto never discovered gold during his 1540 expedition in North Carolina, but anyone who takes a late-evening walk on an exposed sand flat surely will. Cape Lookout National Seashore, where this photo was taken, contains the most extensive sand flats in the state.*

Page 9: *Wide sandy beaches, clear blue skies, and not a soul in sight is a common theme at Cape Lookout National Seashore.*

Title page: *Ring-billed gulls seem to enjoy the sunrises at the Elizabeth City Harbor as much as people do. Of the fourteen species of gulls in the state, ring-bills are among the most common, particularly in winter.*

Title inset: *The John Jackson Hannah cabin in Little Cataloochee Cove of Great Smoky Mountains National Park awaits those who make the 1.2-mile hike on Little Cataloochee Trail. Not as well known as its larger neighbor, Big Cataloochee, Little Cataloochee makes a great destination for those wishing to get away from the Smokies' crowds and blend a little cultural history with their nature walk.*

Opposite page: *Standing sentinel over the Outer Banks since 1872, the Bodie Island Lighthouse has seen many changes. When first built, the lighthouse stood on a true island, then called Body's Island. The National Park Service took ownership of the lighthouse grounds in 1953; in 2000, the U.S. Coast Guard transferred ownership of the historic tower itself.*

Pages 14–15: *Cape Hatteras Lighthouse shines through a foggy morning twilight on Cape Hatteras National Seashore. In 1999, the lighthouse was moved from this vulnerable location near the surf to a safer site a half-mile inland.*

This page: *Some 100 wild horses roam free on Shackleford Banks, a nine-mile-long island within Cape Lookout National Seashore. The horses are the lone descendants from a once-thriving settlement on the island. The last permanent residents left the island in the late 1890s after a severe hurricane had struck. The diet of the wild horses on Shackleford consists mostly of marsh grass, with an occasional nibble on a few succulent herbs.*

Facing page: *Beachcombers at Cape Lookout National Seashore are often rewarded with prized finds, such as this perfect knobbed whelk,* Busycon carica.

Above: *The rock jetty on the western end of Cape Lookout provides great fishing for those casting either from the surf or from a small boat anchored just offshore.*

Right: *Captain Dave Swain of the High Return sets lines during an offshore fishing excursion. The High Return is one of dozens of charter boats embarking from the Oregon Inlet Fishing Center at Cape Hatteras National Seashore.*

Facing page: *Cape Point at Cape Hatteras National Seashore marks an abrupt change in both wind and water, with the cold waters of the Labrador Current meeting the warm waters of the Gulf Stream. The constantly shifting sands, known as Diamond Shoals, extend into the ocean some twenty miles from the Point and pose such a severe danger to vessels that early mariners referred to the area as the Graveyard of the Atlantic.*

Top: *Thousands of people attend the First Flight Centennial Celebration at Wright Brothers National Memorial, exactly 100 years after the first heavier-than-air flight.*

Above: *The tallest sand dunes on the East coast occur at Jockeys Ridge State Park, providing one of the coast's more popular attractions. During the tourist season, the dunes provide a natural playground for all kinds of fun, whether kite flying, sand boarding, hang gliding, or just walking barefooted through the sand.*

Left: *Dedicated on December 17, 2003, at the First Flight Centennial Celebration, this historically accurate life-size sculpture depicts Orville and Wilbur Wright's first flight. In the distance stands the Wright Brothers Monument atop Big Kill Devil Hill.*

Above: *This aerial view of Cape Hatteras Lighthouse and shoreline illustrates the danger posed by the threatening surf before the lighthouse was moved during summer 1999.*

Above: *The "Move of the Century" started on June 17, 1999, when the Cape Hatteras Lighthouse began its journey along an elaborate rail system to its new resting place, safe from the encroaching sea. More than 20,000 people each day watched the historic twenty-three-day move.*

Facing page: *Herbert C. Bonner Bridge spans the treacherous Oregon Inlet at Cape Hatteras National Seashore. Summer weather patterns on the seashore create spectacular sunrises and sunsets, often with the possibility of rainbows.*

The Elizabeth II, *docked at the Manteo Waterfront on Roanoke Island, is open to the public for historical tours. The vessel is a representation of the sixteenth-century sailing vessels used during Sir Walter Raleigh's expedition to the New World. Visitors can explore the middle deck of the* Elizabeth II *and get a sense of what life was like on a voyage across the Atlantic. Colorful and authentic details make the ship a visual and historical treasure.*

The USS North Carolina *was the first of America's modern warships, seeing action in most major World War II campaigns in the Pacific. Today, the decorated battleship endures as a memorial attraction on the Cape Fear River in Wilmington. The engine room of the* North Carolina *has enough gauges to make an engineer wince; during active duty, someone had to keep constant vigil on these controls.*

Above: *The sky glows orange after the sun sets over Silver Lake on Ocracoke Island. Known to the locals as "The Creek," Silver Lake is the focal point of the quaint Ocracoke Village, originally home mostly to fishermen. Recently, it has been discovered by tourists seeking retreat from the suffocating crowds of the more popular beaches.*

Right: *Cape Point on Cape Hatteras National Seashore is famous for its great surf fishing. On autumn mornings, especially on weekends, you'd better get here early if you want a place from which to cast.*

Facing page: *You don't have to catch any fish to have a memorable experience on an Outer Banks fishing pier.*

Above: *The full moon sets over the Cape Fear River at the Cape Fear Memorial Bridge in Wilmington. The bridge features a unique vertical-lift design allowing the entire central span to rise for the passage of tall ships.*

Facing page: *After dinner at one of Wilmington's fine downtown restaurants, a stroll along the waterfront boardwalk is a perfect way to wrap up the evening.*

Most tourists who visit Wilmington eventually wind up at the colorful and fun junction of Market and Water streets.

Kids love the touch tank at the recently renovated North Carolina Aquarium at Fort Fisher. The tank features live horseshoe crabs, sea stars, urchins, whelks, and other animals that youngsters can pick up and feel. North Carolina's other aquariums are located on Emerald Isle and Roanoke Island.

Above: *An old wooden tugboat slowly passes away on the Cape Fear River in Wilmington.*

Right: *The main attraction for visitors to Orton Plantation Gardens in Winnabow is the gardens of azaleas and camellias, but those who take time to stroll all the paths are rewarded with other scenic vistas. This Chinese Bridge spans a small blackwater slough holding numerous stately bald cypress trees.*

Waves crash against a coquina rock outcrop at Fort Fisher State Recreation Area near Wilmington. Exposed only at low tide, it is the only natural rock outcrop on the North Carolina coast.

A majestic live oak tree, Quercus virginiana, *frames the maritime forest on Shackleford Banks in Cape Lookout National Seashore.*

Below: *The Venus flytrap,* Dionaea muscipula, *grows naturally only within a 100-mile radius of Wilmington. These flytraps were photographed in The Nature Conservancy's Green Swamp Nature Preserve, southeast of Wilmington.*

Below: *The common and scientific names of the praying mantis,* Mantis religiosa, *reflect the carnivorous insect's practice of holding up its powerful front legs, as if in prayer.*

Below: *Carnivorous sundews catch prey by secreting a sticky substance that glues any hapless insects that land on or crawl over them. Various species of sundews occur across the state, with most, like this water sundew,* Drosera intermedia, *growing on the coastal plain.*

Above: *Carnivorous pitcher plants, like these yellow pitcher plants,* Sarracenia flava, *have highly modified leaves that are shaped like pitchers. The leaves hold a liquid "witches' brew" that drowns insects and occasional small frogs.*

Above: *Not all critters that crawl into a pitcher plant's tubes end up being prey. This spider has staked out a spot just above the water at the pitcher's base and is awaiting an easy meal of any insects that happen to fall in.*

Above: *Northern pitcher plants,* Sarracenia purpurea, *have numerous downward-pointing hairs that allow insects to crawl in, but prevent them from crawling back out.*

Soft evening twilight settles over the small coastal town of Beaufort, a popular destination for land-based tourists as well as those arriving by water along the Intracoastal Waterway.

A small island of bald cypress trees in Lake Mattamuskeet is illuminated by evening twilight. At eighteen miles long by six miles wide, Mattamuskeet is the largest natural lake in North Carolina.

40

Above: *Early morning light illuminates a flock of snow geese as they take off from a field in Pea Island National Wildlife Refuge on the Outer Banks.*

Left: *A great blue heron takes a break from stalking prey in Lake Lure and uses an unlikely perch. Popular among boaters, sightseers, swimmers, and fishers, this small mountain lake was the setting for the water scenes in the film* Dirty Dancing.

Facing page: *An old footbridge spans the canal beside U.S. 264 in Alligator River National Wildlife Refuge.*

Garrisoned in 1934, Fort Macon protected the vulnerable Beaufort inlet from attack by hostile nations until the Civil War, when it protected Union Navy ships from the Confederacy. After serving as a federal prison and then garrisoned again in the Spanish-American War, Congress sold the fort to the state of North Carolina in 1924 for one dollar. It became the second state park. Visitors to Fort Macon State Park can tour nearly all of the original structure and see numerous re-creations, such as the commissary storeroom. Fort Macon ranks among the most popular state parks in the system, with more than 1.2 million visits annually.

Above: *A mosaic of more than a dozen individual gardens makes up Tryon Palace Gardens in New Bern, attracting thousands of visitors each spring. The Maude Moore Latham Memorial Garden, pictured here, is the largest and most manicured of the gardens in the complex.*

Facing page: *History and culture permeate the port town of New Bern on the Neuse River. The best time to visit is in early spring, when the downtown area is ablaze with flowers. This redbud tree, Cercis ca-nadensis, frames the Tryon Palace Museum Shop.*

Right: *Ocracoke Village, on the southwestern tip of Ocracoke Island, is accessible only by boat, but draws an increasing number of tourists from spring through fall. Popular attractions are Ocracoke Lighthouse and Silver Lake, both shown in this aerial view.*

Below: *Cable ferries once existed all across North Carolina, but only two remain in operation, both in the northeastern corner of the state. Pictured here is the Sans Souci Ferry over the Cashie River, near Plymouth.*

Facing page: *The historic Mattamuskeet Lodge was constructed in 1916 as a massive pumping station to drain Lake Mattamuskeet. In 1934, the property became part of Mattamuskeet National Wildlife Refuge and the building served as a hunting lodge for next three decades. Listed on the National Register of Historic Places in 1980, the building today awaits structural repairs so that it can be reopened as an environmental educational building.*

A full moon outshines the Currituck Beach Lighthouse in Corolla. The only unpainted lighthouse on the North Carolina coast, it is believed by many to be the most picturesque. Visitors with strong lungs and calf muscles can climb to the top of the lighthouse using a spiraling series of 214 steps. The view from the top is worth all the huffing and puffing.

Dawn paints a colorful sky that reflects in the Pasquotank River at the Elizabeth City Harbor. The harbor is a popular stopping point for travelers along the Intracoastal Waterway.

Above: *Early morning sunlight shines on the dew-covered wiregrass of a longleaf pine savanna in The Nature Conservancy's Green Swamp Nature Preserve in Brunswick County.*

Left: *Bald cypress trees,* Taxodium distichum, *line the primitive shoreline of Lake Phelps in Pettigrew State Park in Washington County. In addition to huge cypress trees, the park contains at least seven state champion trees of other species.*

Facing page: *A November sunset on Lake Mattamuskeet in Hyde County is a magical time when thousands of waterfowl are silhouetted against orange skies.*

Above: *Completed in 1840, the Greek Revival–style North Carolina State Capitol is a National Historic Landmark. All branches of state government operated from the building until the 1880s, when the first branches of government began moving to other headquarters. Today, the building serves as a museum and offices for the governor.*

Left: *The Senate Chamber in the North Carolina State Capitol hasn't entertained a political debate since 1963, the year the General Assembly moved to the State Legislative Building. Today, the chamber and other rooms of the building entertain the public with free, self-guided tours.*

Facing page: *Although modern tobacco curing systems have largely made obsolete the traditional method of curing in barns, scenes like this are common in rural western North Carolina during autumn. This barn is in the Valle Crucis region of Watauga County.*

Above: *The North Carolina Museum of Natural Sciences houses four floors of exhibits, with one of the most popular ones being the Prehistoric North Carolina exhibit. This life-size cast of a Tyrannosaurus rex skull opens the display, creating an irresistible opportunity for children to touch the past.*

Right: *An ancient habitat is recreated in the Prehistoric North Carolina exhibit of the North Carolina Museum of Natural Sciences.*

Facing page: *The Benjamin N. Duke Flentrop Organ in the Duke University Chapel contains 5,000 pipes. Installed in 1976, the organ is regularly played for Sunday services.*

Above: *While the adults enjoy musical performances at MerleFest, the kids take in their own shows, such as the Flea Circus.*

Above: *Historic Bost Grist Mill in Cabarrus County is decorated for Christmas. Built in the early 1800s, the restored mill is on the National Register of Historic Places and features original milling equipment and artifacts.*

Facing page: *At MerleFest in Wilkesboro, Doc Watson strums a guitar and belts out a tune like only he can. Named after Watson's son Merle, who was killed in a tractor accident, the annual gathering of bluegrass, blues, and country music performers attracts thousands of visitors from around the globe.*

Above: *Children love the hands-on experience of the Touch and Learn Center at the North Carolina Zoological Park in Asheboro.*

Left: *North Carolina native and stock car legend Richard Petty—"King Richard" to his followers—displays decades of racing memorabilia at his museum in Randleman. Featured are several original stock cars, including Richard's famous 1970 Plymouth Superbird.*

Above: *A panther statue guards the Bank of America Stadium, home of the Carolina Panthers.*

Right: *The Carolina Panthers take to the field for a contest with the Detroit Lions at Bank of America Stadium in Charlotte. The Panthers won the game and went on to play in the 2004 Super Bowl.*

The modern skyline of Charlotte looms over Marshall Park. In addition to the skyscraper view, the park features three memorials: the Holocaust Memorial, the Monument of Valor, and the Martin Luther King Memorial Statue. Charlotte is the country's second-largest banking center, boasting the headquarters for two of the nation's largest banks. Both the Bank of America Corporate Center, the tallest building in the Carolinas at 871 feet, and One Wachovia Center, the second-tallest, are visible.

Above: *The exterior of Duke Energy's Charlotte headquarters features an eighty-square-foot neon light sculpture named Quadrille. The artwork contains several hours of randomly selected animations, so viewers rarely see the same pattern twice.*

Left: *Famed artist Ben Long created one of the largest secular frescoes in the world in the lobby of the Bank of America headquarters in Charlotte. The three separate panels, called a triptych, have individual but related themes. This panel's theme is* Chaos/Creativity.

Above: *A buck-rail fence frames the Single Brothers' Workshop in Old Salem. The building is a reconstruction of the original 1771 structure.*

Left: *A cobblestone sidewalk fronts the T. Bagge Merchant building in Old Salem.*

Facing page: *A winter snow, red paint, and an azure sky create a study of contrasts in the historic Moravian village of Old Salem in Winston-Salem. Established in 1766, Old Salem is one of the most authentic living history restorations in America and attracts visitors year round.*

Above: *No longer needed to grind corn, this old water wheel from a western North Carolina tub mill lies in picturesque decay.*

Facing page: *Originally intended to be only advertisement for a Tennessee tourist attraction, the Rock City barns scattered across the rural South eventually became more popular than the attraction itself. While most of the 900 or so barns no longer exist or have fallen into disrepair, a few still stand and continue to advertise, including this one just outside of Bryson City.*

Dewdrops glisten on a spider web attached to an old barbed-wire fence in the Smokies.

Fans of The Andy Griffith Show *flock to Mount Airy—Griffith's hometown and inspiration for the fictional Mayberry—to tour the many sites made popular in the show. Squad Car Tours, based at Wally's Service on Main Street, guide visitors around town in a vintage 1962 replica of the show's squad car.*

Top: *Who says Texas has the biggest cows in the nation? No animal in America can compete with this behemoth residing on a Henderson County farm.*

Above: *Vines grow on the idle gas pumps at the former Jones Grocery Store in Yadkin County.*

Left: *This detailed replica of an old general store stands in the apple country of Henderson County.*

Above: *Visitors climb Temple Mound at Town Creek Indian Mound Historic Site. Situated on a bluff near the junction of Town Creek and Little River in Montgomery County, the ceremonial center was the hub for religious, social, and political activities of the Pee Dee Indians.*

Facing page: *All the structures at Town Creek Indian Mound have been re-created, the originals having long ago disappeared. This scene shows the interior of the Temple Mound.*

Above: *More than 250 miles of the Blue Ridge Parkway's 469 miles traverse the high mountains of North Carolina, providing access to incomparable scenic views. A great place to watch the sunset is from the Cowee Mountains Overlook, picture here at milepost 430.7.*

Left: *Crepuscular rays bathe the Cowee Mountains as seen from the Blue Ridge Parkway near Richland Balsam.*

Storm clouds glow with the colors of sunset in this view from Grassy Ridge in the Roan Mountain Highlands region of Pisgah National Forest.

Above: *A classic Appalachian scene of layered mountains as far as the eye can see. This view is from Round Bald in the Roan Mountain Highlands of Pisgah National Forest.*

Left: *Elk,* Cervus elaphus, *are once again roaming the Smokies, after having been reintroduced into Cataloochee Cove in early 2001.*

Above: *Cherohala Scenic Skyway winds its way down the mountain in this early morning view. The Skyway links Robbinsville, North Carolina, with Tellico Plains, Tennessee, offering spectacular scenery, hiking, waterfalls, and wildflower viewing.*

Facing page: *The open, grassy top of Round Bald in Pisgah National Forest provides an unforgettable camping experience when the weather cooperates. More often than not, the mountain is bathed in dense clouds and fog.*

The original Mast General Store in Valle Crucis has been in near-continuous operation since 1883 and for the last few decades has been a popular tourist attraction. Shoppers can purchase just about anything, from lye soap to blue jeans to hammocks.

Above: *In a tradition going back to the late 1800s, local old-timers play bottle-cap checkers by the old wood stove in the Mast General Store.*

Left: *An official U.S. Post Office resides inside the Mast General Store. When a customer needs postal assistance, the store employee switches roles from clerk to postmaster.*

Above: *Flat Top Manor overlooks Bass Lake near the resort town of Blowing Rock. Once the country estate of textile baron Moses H. Cone, the manor and surrounding grounds are now among the most popular attractions in the Blue Ridge Parkway system.*

Facing page: *The Colonial Revival architecture of Flat Top Manor has attracted interest since its completion in 1901. The 1999 film* The Green Mile *featured the manor as a retirement home for the movie's main character. Visitors at Flat Top Manor can also enjoy a leisurely rock while taking in the magnificent views.*

An early morning breeze blows the grass on Gregory Bald in Great Smoky Mountains National Park. The bald is world famous for its June display of wild azaleas.

Left: *The roots of a sycamore,* Platanus occidentalis, *fan out over the floodplain of Big Creek in Great Smoky Mountains National Park.*

Below: *Tuckasegee River Gorge in Nantahala National Forest receives few visitors due to the extremely difficult hike required to access it. The rewards for the hardy few who make the trek are spectacular views along the potholed stream.*

This row, top to bottom: *Catawba rhododendron*, Rhododendron catawbiense. *Bull thistle*, Cirsium vulgare. *Painted trillium*, Trillium undulatum.

This row, top to bottom: *Grass of Parnassus*, Parnassia asarifolia. *Gray's lily*, Lilium grayi. *Dense blazing star*, Liatris spicata.

This row, top to bottom: *Deptford pink*, Dianthus armeria. *Black-eyed Susan*, Rudbeckia hirta. *Indian paint brush*, Castilleja coccinea.

This row, top to bottom: *Eastern blue-eyed grass*, Sisyrinchium atlanticum. *Wild monkshood*, Aconitum uncinatum. *Crested dwarf iris*, Iris cristata.

Red poppies grow beside I-77 in Surry County, part of the North Carolina Roadside Wildflower Program. Begun on twelve acres in 1985, it is today the largest and most successful wildflower program in the country, consisting of more than 3,000 roadside acres from the mountains to the sea.

Above: *The spectacular Grandfather Trail leads hikers along the jagged crest of Grandfather Mountain. The trail is so rugged that it requires hikers to use ladders and cables to get over, around, and even under the rocks.*

Facing page: *Chimney Rock Park has attracted tourists for nearly a century. The most popular feature of the park is the chimney overlooking Hickorynut Gorge and Lake Lure. Other features include the 404-foot Hickorynut Falls.*

Right: A stone observation tower stands atop Mount Mitchell in Mount Mitchell State Park, North Carolina's first park. Beneath the tower is the grave of Dr. Elisha Mitchell, who, in the 1830s and 1840s, was the first person to measure the mountain's elevation and determine that it is the highest in the East. Dr. Mitchell died in 1857 after falling over what is now called Mitchell Falls, located on the same mountain.

Below: Among the most popular whitewater rivers in the south, Nantahala River in Swain County is an eight-mile course of Class I and II rapids, culminating in the Class III Nantahala Falls, being maneuvered by this excited couple.

Father and son enjoy a slide down Sliding Rock on Looking Glass Creek in Pisgah National Forest. An average of 11,000 gallons of water a minute propel thrill seekers down the sixty-foot slope into the bone-chilling pool below.

Above: *A mossy footlog spans Indian Creek on Martins Gap Trail, in the Deep Creek section of Great Smoky Mountains National Park.*

Facing page: *Little Cataloochee Baptist Church in the remote Little Cataloochee Cove of Great Smoky Mountains National Park is reached by a two-mile hike.*

The Zebulon B. Vance Birthplace in Weaverville memorializes one of North Carolina's favorite sons. Vance served his native state from 1854 to 1894 (the year of his death) as a U.S. congressman, soldier, governor, and finally U.S. senator.

Above: *The weaving room at Zebulon B. Vance Birthplace occupies a small detached building behind the main house.*

Left: *The kitchen and dining room at Zebulon B. Vance Birthplace are ready for service.*

Above: *October in Great Smoky Mountains National Park is a magical time. This view is from the transmountain New-found Gap Road, which runs from Cherokee, North Carolina, to Gatlinburg, Tennessee.*

Left: *One of the best places to view the sunrise in Great Smoky Mountains National Park is from the parking lot near the summit of Clingmans Dome, the highest peak in the park at 6,643 feet. The dead trees are Fraser firs that have succumbed to acid rain and to a nonnative pest called the balsam woolly adelgid.*

Facing page: *Views along Cherohala Scenic Skyway in Graham County are especially glorious during autumn.*

Above: *A lighted cross overlooks Lake Junaluska near Waynesville. The lake and surrounding grounds are home to the Lake Junaluska Conference & Retreat Center of the United Methodist Church.*

Facing page: *A moderate 0.6-mile hike leads to the John Wasilik Memorial Tree in Nantahala National Forest. With a circumference of more than 26 feet and a height of 135 feet (before being topped by a storm), the tree is considered the second-largest yellow poplar in the nation.*

Mount Jefferson looms in the distance of this wintry landscape in rural Ashe County.

September provides a different view from same vantage point as in the previous photograph.

You never know what you'll find at a Franklin gem mine, as one lucky prospector discovered when he washed the mud off this 300-carat ruby.

Nine-year-old Angela Booth searches for treasures at a Franklin gem mine.

Above: *At the Mining Museum of Emerald Village near Little Switzerland, visitors can enter the mining shaft and explore original mining artifacts.*

Facing page: *The popular Great Smoky Mountains Railroad offers numerous excursions on routes from Dillsboro to Bryson City and from Bryson City to the Nantahala Outdoor Center in Wesser. Here, the steam engine crosses the old iron trestle over Tuckasegee River.*

Above: *Once a common sight across western North Carolina, most small general stores have decayed or fallen victim to the bulldozer. This store, though long closed, still stands in the community of Luck, in Madison County.*

Facing page: *Carl Sandberg's home in Flat Rock is a National Historic Site. Visitors can tour the grounds free or take a guided tour of the home for a small fee.*

Above: *Typical of scenes along the state's northern portion of the Blue Ridge Parkway, this pasture is in Julian Price Memorial Park, near Blowing Rock.*

Facing page: *A dewy spider web is anchored to wingstem,* Verbesina alternifolia.

Roan Mountain is known worldwide for its spectacular display of Catawba rhodo-dendron. This fence runs along the base of Round Bald, part of the Roan Mountain Highlands.

The longleaf pine, Pinus palustris, *is North Carolina's state tree.*

Above: *A deep snow envelopes a rural farm in Ashe County.*

Facing page: *A light dusting of snow covers Whitewater Falls in Nantahala National Forest.*

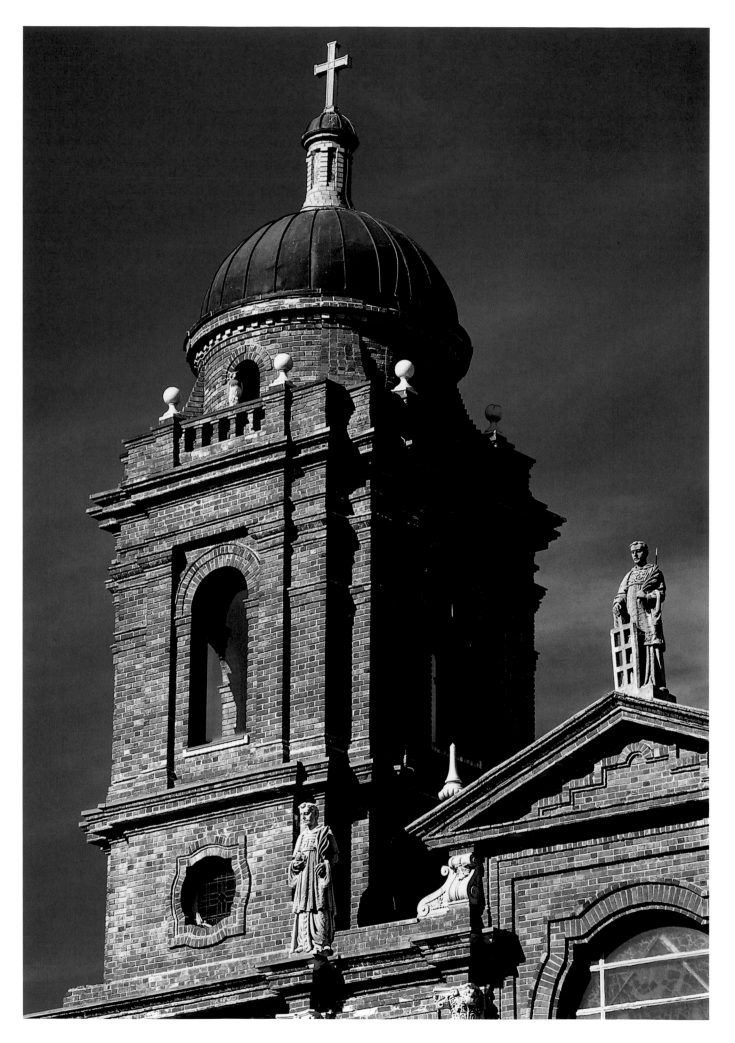

Above: *The resort town of Asheville has been popular among vacationers since the late 1700s.*

Facing page: *The Basilica of St. Lawrence in Asheville, with its unique dome and Spanish Renaissance architecture, is considered the "Mother church of western North Carolina."*

Above: *The 40,000-square-foot spa at Asheville's Grove Park Inn features a subter-ranean design with stone walls, arches, waterfalls, and two large pools.*

Facing page: *Eclectic Wall Street in downtown Asheville features the Flat Iron sculpture sitting in front of the Flat Iron Building.*

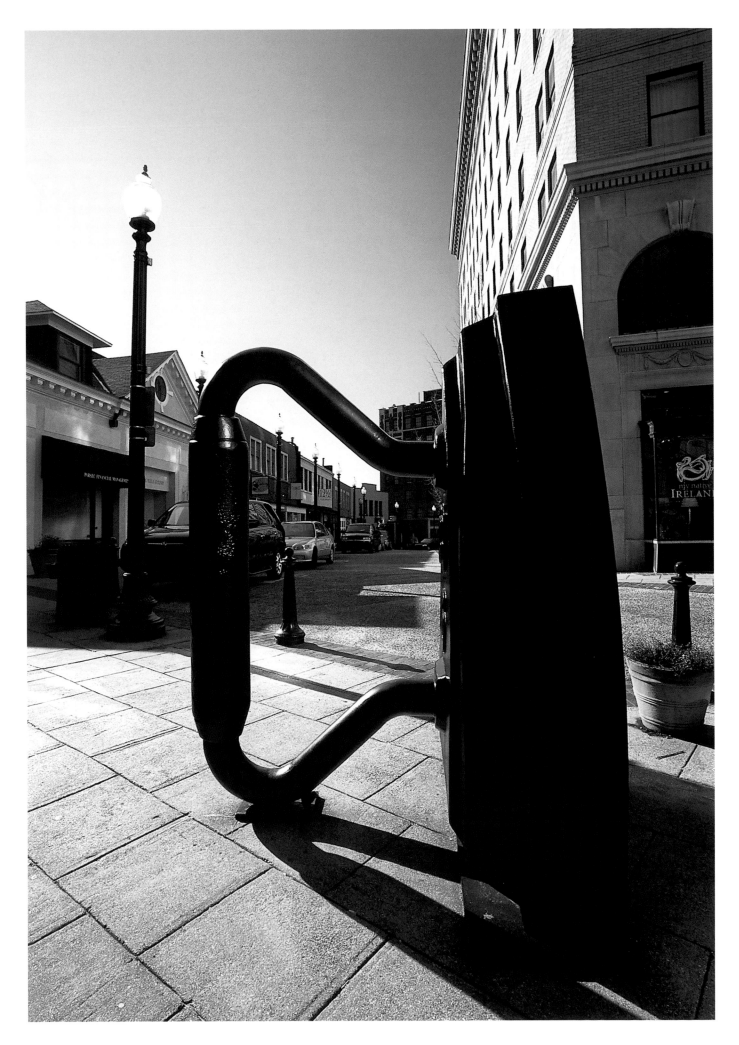

George W. Vanderbilt's Biltmore House in Asheville is America's largest private home, boasting four acres of floor space. Completed in 1895, the French Renaissance–inspired chateau is today a National Historic Landmark and among the most popular tourist destinations in the Southeast.

Lavender wisteria and tulips of all shades grace the gardens at Biltmore in spring.

Above: *Tours at Shelton Vineyards in Dobson take visitors inside the Barrel Cave where they can sip wines right out of the barrel.*

Facing page: *The clock tower at Biltmore Estate Winery is part of the original dairy.*

Fontana Lake, forming the southwestern border of Great Smoky Mountains National Park, has some 400 houseboats floating on it, providing owners with year-round recreational opportunities.

Above: *The sun shines through the trees along Toxaway River in Gorges State Park, Transylvania County.*

Left: *At 480 feet, Fontana Dam on the Little Tennessee River is the tallest dam east of the Rocky Mountains.*

Opened in 1997 and operated by the Eastern Band of Cherokee Indians, Harrah's Cherokee Casino is North Carolina's only gambling resort.

Thunder claps and lightning flashes when someone hits it big at Harrah's.

Above: *Oconaluftee Indian Village in Cherokee re-creates the life of the Cherokee Indian through demonstrations and displays, such as this typical nineteenth-century Cherokee dwelling.*

Facing page: *A native Cherokee woman demonstrates beadwork at Oconaluftee Indian Village.*

Following page: *Sunlight is mirrored on distant lakes in this view from Standing Indian Mountain in Nantahala National Forest.*